Lynda Field has a degree in sociology and social psychology. A trained counsellor and psychotherapist specializing in personal and group development, she lives in Essex, England

by the same author

60 Ways to Change Your Life
60 Ways to Feel Amazing
Creating Self-Esteem
The Self-Esteem Workbook
Self-Esteem for Women

Lynda Field's 60 Tips for Self-Esteem

Quick Ways to Boost Your Confidence

LYNDA FIELD

E L E M E N T

Shaftesbury, Dorset • Boston, Massachusetts
Melbourne, Victoria

DEDICATED TO MY SON JACK PORTER
who can always find something good to say about
everybody

© Element Books Limited 1997
Text © Lynda Field 1997

First published in Great Britain in 1997 by
Element Books Limited
Shaftesbury, Dorset SP7 8BP

Published in the USA in 1997 by
Element Books, Inc.
160 North Washington Street, Boston, MA 02114

Published in Australia in 1997 by
Element Books
and distributed by Penguin Australia Limited
487 Maroondah Highway, Ringwood, Victoria 3134

Reprinted 1998 (Twice)
Reprinted 1999

Illustrations by Alison Campbell
Cover design by Mark Slader
Page design by Roger Lightfoot
Typeset by Bournemouth Colour Press, Parkstone, Poole
Printed and bound in Great Britain by
Creative Print and Design Wales, Ebbw Vale

British Library Cataloguing in Publication
data available

Library of Congress Cataloging in Publication data
Field, Lynda.
    [60 tips for self-esteem]
    Lynda Field's 60 tips for self-esteem : quick ways to boost your
confidence / Lynda Field.
        p.   cm.
    Includes bibliographical references and index.
    ISBN 1–86204–103–2 (alk. paper)
    1. Self-esteem.   2. Self-confidence.   I. Title.
BF697.5.S46F53   1997
158.1—dc21   97–1927
                                                              CI

ISBN 1–86204–103–2

Contents

Introduction

Self-esteem is the vital ingredient for success and happiness in our lives. When we have it we feel good about ourselves, we feel calm, confident and in control and everything is possible. When we lose it we know immediately, our self-belief disappears and everything starts to go wrong.

When I was researching and writing my books on self-esteem I talked to hundreds of people about the quality of their lives. It seems that *everyone* is looking self-esteem and that even the most confident-looking people can and do suffer from self-doubt.

A very successful woman with a close family and a thriving business said this about herself:

> My self-esteem come and goes. I can be feeling really great one minute and on top of the world, and then something happens and I react badly and the next moment my self-esteem has gone. It happens very quickly and when it does I feel useless and no good and I don't know what to do to lift myself up again.

It seems that this sudden loss of self-esteem is common to everyone. We all need to know what we can do to 'lift ourselves up again' when things go wrong and we lose our self-belief. This little book answers that need. If you would like a deeper understanding of the theory behind these tips then refer to my books, *Creating Self-Esteem*, *The Self-Esteem Workbook* and *Self-Esteem for Women*.

In *Lynda Field's 60 Tips for Self-Esteem* you will find a whole range of quick, simple and practical methods which you can use immediately. There are many ways to create self-esteem, so use this book to choose the ones that suit you best.

Say positive things about yourself

1   Say positive things about yourself

Listen to the ways that people talk about themselves. It's so common to hear things like:

- 'I'm no good.'
- 'I'm useless.'
- 'Trust me to make a mess of it.'
- 'I can't do that.'

If people speak negatively about themselves and are continually bringing themselves down it doesn't take long before we are agreeing with them. If you wanted someone to help you with a project, would you ask a person who kept telling you how useless they were? Could you trust someone who told you that they always made a mess of things?

When we bring ourselves down our self-esteem falls lower and lower. Don't speak badly about yourself. Instead of saying something negative about yourself say something positive.

EXAMPLES

Replace		'I can't.'
	with	'I'll do the best I can.'
Replace		'I always make a mess of things.'
	with	'I always learn from my mistakes.'
Replace		'I'm no good at . . .'
	with	'I am getting better at . . .'

When you say positive things about yourself you increase your self-respect and so others treat you with respect, which in turn increases your self-esteem.

Change a poor self- image

2 Change a poor self-image

We have all experienced this. We wake up on a bad day, look in the mirror and think 'Oh, what a state! I look so old/tired/wrinkly/fat . . .', and that poor self-image stays with us all day. Poor self-image means low self-esteem.

What can we do about this? Start to appreciate something about your appearance. Look for something that you can like about yourself, however small it may be. Appreciate a toe, your eyelashes, a fingernail. Begin to admire an aspect of your appearance and you will gradually learn how to appreciate other things about yourself.

As you start to appreciate your body your self-image will improve and so will your self-esteem. You will feel more confident and this will be reflected in the way you look. A good self-image creates self-esteem.

Stay away from grumpy people

3 Stay away from grumpy people

Do you know people who are always complaining? About the weather; the crime rate; that awful disaster; their illnesses; the way they have been badly treated; the rotten politicians; the terrible state of the world, etc. We all know people like this and we know how it feels to spend time with them. I'm not talking about those who are genuinely low and need our help, I'm talking about those people whose life work seems to be to bring other people down.

You may be feeling great, high in self-esteem and full of positive ideas . . . and then you meet Mr or Mrs or Ms Grumpy. The conversation becomes more and more terrible and you may even start to feel guilty about feeling so good. Get away! This person is determined that they (and you) will never have a good day. They are victims of life and they want to stay that way. Protect your positive feelings and self-esteem and stay away from grumpy people.

Be your own best friend

4 Be your own best friend

So many times people have told me how much they hate themselves when they are feeling low in self-esteem. They criticize themselves for their behaviour, for mistakes they have made and for their inability to make decisions. When we are low in self-esteem this self-hate just takes us even lower.

When you are really low, try this wonderful technique which can lift you out of your negativity.

EXERCISE

Become your own best friend. Imagine that you have stepped out of your own body and that you are now standing next to yourself. (Don't think too much about this, just use your imagination.) Now look at yourself. What can you say that is comforting and helpful? How can you encourage this person to feel more confident about him or herself? What would you say to your best friend? Perhaps you would put your arm around her and tell her that she's doing really well and that you appreciate all her good qualities. Talk to yourself the way you would to your very best friend.

This technique is so simple and so effective. Become your own best friend and your self-esteem will immediately increase.

Change your negative self-beliefs

5 Change your negative self-beliefs

When you look at your reflection, what sort of person do you see? This is a hard thing to do, especially on a day when you are feeling low. We are so self-critical, we treat ourselves badly and can find so many things 'wrong' with ourselves. Most of the negative beliefs we hold about ourselves have no foundation in reality. We are not really selfish, unkind, cruel, lazy, thoughtless, stupid, no good, worthless . . . etc. (I am sure that you can add your own personal favourites to this list.) We learned our beliefs about ourselves at a very early age when we believed literally everything that we heard.

If, for example, I was told that I was stupid when I was very small, I may still hold that belief even now. I may be very clever, but deep down I will believe that I am stupid. This belief will affect my whole life. I will always doubt my abilities until I change my negative beliefs.

We change our negative beliefs about ourselves by training our minds to believe positive things instead. It really is very simple. For example, instead of carrying on believing that 'I am stupid' (which keeps me low in self-esteem) I will contradict this belief by making the following positive affirmation:

AFFIRMATION: I am intelligent.

Make a positive affirmation for yourself. Say it as many times as you can remember. Write it on the wall. Sing it in the bath. Keep on saying it until you believe it. Eventually your positive affirmation will replace your negative belief.

Affirmations work! Just keep making them. What have you got to lose? Only a lifetime of negativity and low self-esteem.

Look forward and not back

6 Look forward and not back

Do you recognize any of these thoughts?

- If only I had not done that.
- I wish that I had said something else.
- I should have behaved differently.
- I regret doing that.
- If only I could do it all over again.

They often come to us in the small hours of the morning when we have time to ponder our difficulties. We have all lain there in the dark worrying and blaming ourselves for what has happened and wishing that we had done something different.

We can all look back and regret our actions but *we cannot change the past*, and if we continue to agonize over what we should and shouldn't have done our lives will be miserable and we will be very low in self-esteem.

Stop blaming yourself and let go of the past. Remember that you did the very best that you could at the time and now look forward towards a positive future.

Stop being a victim

7 Stop being a victim

Do you ever feel you are being taken for granted by people? This might be because you are doing things that you really don't want to do but you just can't say 'no'. For example, if your friend keeps asking you to look after her noisy children after school *and you don't want to*, then the next time she asks you, just say 'no'. I am sure that you can find your own personal example of this sort of behaviour. Think carefully about why you are allowing yourself to be used in this way and then *act* to change the situation.

If you always do the washing up and the cleaning then your family will always expect you to do it. Give your family members some jobs to do around the house. Teach your children how to clean their own rooms. Don't become a slave in your own home. You are not a victim with low self-esteem unless you are choosing to be one.

Throw out your old clothes

8   Throw out your old clothes

Our clothes can be so much part of our image. Have you any clothes in your closet that you haven't worn for a couple of years? If you have, ask yourself why you are hanging on to them.

Are you keeping things because of past memories? If so you may be unable to move forward in your life because you are feeling stuck in the past. If this is the case then get rid of these clothes.

Perhaps you are waiting to 'grow back' into some clothes. So many people have a whole range of clothes that are too small for them, and they keep them for that time when they will have lost enough weight for them all to fit again. If this is you, get rid of these clothes. Every time you open your closet to see the trousers and dresses and all the other things that are too small, you are affecting your own body image. They are a constant reminder that you haven't lost the weight you had hoped to lose.

Living the past (whether it was a slimmer past or not) is not good for your feelings of self-respect and self-worth. Do yourself and your self-esteem a favour – throw out these clothes or, better still, give them to someone who will wear them. Take your old gear to the local charity shop and clear out your closet and your mind of the old memories that hold you back.

Take some time just for yourself

9   Take some time just for yourself

Do you ever find that you just don't seem to have any time for yourself? This seems to be more of a problem for women than for men. Women are more likely to be trying to do everything: running a home, being a mother, being a wife and probably working as well. It's no wonder that we often have no time for ourselves.

Do something *just* for yourself. Go to that evening class; go to the hairdressers; go for a swim. What would you love to do but never seem to have the time for? Make the time! When you look after yourself in this way you are recognizing that your needs are as important as everyone else's and so you increase your self-worth and self-esteem.

Do what you've got to do

10   Do what you've got to do

Think of something that you need to do but that you keep putting off for some reason. Most of us have a long list of jobs that we continually think about doing but never actually seem to do. Make a list of these jobs.

THINGS I NEED TO DO

1 ....

2 ....

3 ....

Make a full list even if it is very long. Now choose one thing on the list and *do it*! I can guarantee that you will feel as if you have really accomplished something once you have done this job. You may even feel inspired to tackle something else on your list.

When we know that we have things to do but keep finding excuses not to do them we begin to lose our self-respect. This can easily create a cycle where we begin to doubt our ability to do *anything* and this negative thinking leads to low self-esteem. We can spend much more energy thinking about doing something and then not doing it and then not liking ourselves for not doing it than it takes to actually do it.

You can easily break this cycle. Next time you hear yourself saying, 'I really need to clean out that cupboard; mend that skirt; write that letter; fill in that form; make that phone call; pull out those weeds . . . etc. – *just do it*!

Make an assertive phone call

11 Make an assertive phone call

If you feel ill at ease using the phone or you have a particularly difficult call to make, do it standing up. The person you are phoning is most likely to be sitting down. Although you can't see the person that you are talking to and they can't see you, you will feel at a physical and psychological advantage. Sounds too simple to be of any use? Try it, it really works!

Smile into the phone. Sounds crazy? When you smile, you sound more confident and assertive and people treat you with more respect. Smiling also increases your feelings of well-being, so maybe that phone call will not be as frightening an experience as you are expecting.

Eat well for a day

12 Eat well for a day

If we put the wrong sort of petrol in our car it won't fire well on all cylinders. The same applies to human beings. If we eat things that are unsuitable for us we will not feel our best, look our best or perform at our best.

Decide to eat well for a day. Take charge of your food intake and become aware of what you are putting into your body. Make sure that you eat plenty of fresh vegetables and fruit as well as some protein. Eat wholemeal carbohydrates and avoid sugar, alcohol, caffeine and excessive fats. Drink lots of water and cleanse your system.

Eating sensibly for a day is a great way to boost your self-esteem. If you have been eating anything and everything without thought, then breaking bad habits even just for a day will demonstrate that you have the strength to control yourself and to take in the very best nutrients for your body. Eating well may even turn into a habit and that can only increase your feelings of general well-being and self-esteem.

Ask yourself 'Does it really matter?'

13 Ask yourself 'Does it really matter?'

Whenever you feel yourself getting annoyed or upset about something, ask yourself this question, 'Does it really matter?' If it does then be sure to express your feelings to the right person. However, very often we allow ourselves to become worked up about something that really doesn't matter, and then our irritation can quickly lead us into low self-esteem.

Your child has dropped chocolate on her dress; your partner didn't put the dishes away in *exactly* the right place; the house is not perfectly tidy. Is it worth making a point? Is it worth getting upset?

When we are feeling good about ourselves these minor details are unimportant. When we are feeling low the small things really seem to matter. The next time that you become annoyed with some minor detail, think again. Ask yourself, 'Does it really matter?' and if the answer is 'no' then say to yourself, 'This doesn't really matter', let go and move on.

Clear your mind

14 Clear your mind

We are more than our minds. We are mind, body and spirit. Sometimes it seems that we are so busy thinking things and doing things that we can never truly relax. We can only really feel at peace when we are contacting the spiritual part of our nature, and for this we need to clear our minds.

EXERCISE

Sit comfortably with your eyes closed and watch your mind at work; just let it wander. Notice how full of thoughts you are! Ignore them, they will keep coming, just take no notice of them. Concentrate on the rhythm of your breathing. Follow your in-breath and then your out-breath. Be aware of your breath. As you breathe in think 'in' and as you breathe out think 'out'. So in, out, in, out. Each time your mind wanders off, follow it, observe that it has wandered and then come back to your breathing. Become aware of the place *between* the breaths – when you are not breathing in and not breathing out. Now concentrate on this place. Move your awareness to this place between the in- and the out-breath. When your mind wanders off, follow it and bring it back to this place between the breaths. After a few minutes let your thoughts return, wriggle your hands and feet and open your eyes.

You will feel refreshed and so much more! We can only be high in self-esteem if we are balanced in mind, body and spirit. Clear your mind and free your spirit regularly, and your life will change for the better.

Say what you mean

15   Say what you mean

People often say to me that their biggest problem is that they never seem to get what they want: life treats them badly and people treat them badly, so how can they feel good about themselves?

Well, we can only get what we want if we ask for what we want. This may seem to be obvious and yet we often don't ask for what we want because we don't always say what we mean. Have you ever had a conversation like this?

'Let's go out to eat tonight.'	(you – wanting to go on to an Indian restaurant)
'OK.'	(partner)
'Where do you want to go?'	(you)
'I don't care.'	(partner)
'Well let's decide on somewhere.'	(you)
'I don't care, wherever you want.'	(partner)
'Well let's decide on somewhere.'	(you)
'I don't care, wherever you want.'	(partner)
'No, you decide'.	(you)
'OK, let's go for a pizza.'	(partner)
'OK.'	(you – 'As usual, I never get my way.')

Next time you don't get what you want, check that you asked for it clearly. Did you say what you meant or did you hold back for some reason? Start saying exactly what you mean and asking for what you want. Your feelings of self-respect will increase, and you will have much more chance of getting what you want.

Smile and the world smiles with you

16 Smile and the world smiles with you

When our self-esteem is low we look low and we find it difficult to communicate with others because we are all tied up in feeling bad about ourselves.

Sometimes we can break this cycle by changing something very simple – like a facial expression. A smile can break a negative cycle of:

- feeling low in self-esteem
- looking dejected and feeling unable to communicate with others
- others stopping communicating with us
- enhanced feelings of low self-esteem (you see, I'm so worthless that people don't bother with me any more).

Look in the mirror and smile. Really smile with all of your face – eyes as well as mouth. Look closely at your smile; it lights up your face. Take your smile for a walk, practise it in the presence of others – the effect can be quite dramatic. The smiling habit helps you to look *outside* of yourself, and sometimes this is all you need to trigger a change in your low feelings and to increase your self-esteem.

Never mind the weather

17   Never mind the weather

I was phoning a colleague and I asked him if he had a good day. 'Oh no,' he replied, 'the weather here has been terrible. It's been raining all day.' My friend works in an office and he has a car so he didn't need to get wet, yet the rain had ruined his day.

As I am writing this we are in mid-summer, the sun is hot and we are having what many of us call 'beautiful weather'. This same friend is telling me now that he is too hot and that it's too muggy. This man is a severe victim of the weather!

Have you ever been upset about the temperature, the rain, the fog, the sun . . . and so on?

We cannot change the weather.

Don't allow yourself to become victimized by something that you cannot change – this is a classic case of self-victimization. Never mind the weather. Get on and enjoy your life.

Take a risk

18   Take a risk

Sometimes we really want to make a change in our lives but we are afraid to take the next step because it feels too risky. Perhaps we want to stand up to someone because they are victimizing us. We might want to train for a new job or begin a new relationship.

What is it that you would like to do to change your life in some way? What are the risks involved?

If we want to make something happen we must dare to change the way we behave, and this means being able to ask for want we want. Daring to change may involve the possible risks of:

- failing
- being rejected
- being laughed at
- people not liking us any more.

Ask yourself if these things really matter to you.

If you never take a risk you will never get what you want and you will be low in self-esteem. Make something happen, however small. Take the risk, and your self-esteem will soar.

Tell someone how much you appreciate them

19 Tell someone how much you appreciate them

A man I know told me that he had spent his whole life trying to make his father proud of him. He had followed the same profession and the same football team and even lived in the same street. Although this man was married with his own children he was always waiting for his father to acknowledge his achievements. When his father became very ill my friend spent a lot of time at his bedside. One day, not long before his death, the old man said this to his son: 'My boy, you have always been a marvellous son and I am so proud of you.' My friend burst into tears as he heard the words that he had been waiting for all his life.

Don't hold back on your appreciation for people. Give credit where it is due and enjoy the feeling that it brings. Who do you appreciate in your life? Have you told them? If not, then tell them. When we show our appreciation for others they feel increased self-esteem and so do we! Whenever you help another person to feel better about themselves, then you will also feel better about yourself.

Stop blaming yourself

20   Stop blaming yourself

Self-blame encourages low self-esteem and does nothing to improve any situation.

So what if you burned the dinner or forgot to keep a dentist's appointment? These things are not the end of the world and certainly not worth punishing yourself for.

If you feel that you have behaved badly or made a serious mistake then apologize and try to put the situation right. When you have done the best you can, that is indeed the best you can do. Accept the blame and then let go. Let yourself off the hook. We all make lots of mistakes. Learn from them and then move on.

Associate with successful people

21 Associate with successful people

Do you admire your friends and colleagues, or are you associating with victims? Many people with low confidence levels actually feel threatened by people who appear to be successful and so choose to spend time with people who are in an even worse situation than themselves. Check your motives:

- Are you friends with that poor helpless person because you are really trying to help her to change her situation?
- Are you really helping her?
- Does she want to be helped?
- Are you enjoying feeling sorry for her?
- Do you feel more confident when you are with her because at least you are more together than she is?

If we choose to spend time with people who cannot handle success we will become just like them.

Look for people who have gone before you and have made a success of whatever you are trying to achieve. Whatever you are trying to improve – your relationship, career, personal development, dress sense, parenting, etc. – check out people who have been successful in your chosen area and learn from them.

Success attracts success, just as negativity attracts more negativity. Mix with people you admire and you will feel inspired to create your own success, and of course your self-esteem can only increase.

Draw your line in the sand

22   Draw your line in the sand

Imagine that someone needs your help. They want you to do something for them but you have already planned an outing with some friends.

What will you do? If you say 'yes' and abandon your own plans, are you being a good friend or are you being a victim?

Sometimes it can be very hard to decide whether your needs come before or after the needs of someone else. Every situation is different, but there is a process that you can use to help you to decide exactly how far you will go for someone else, or in other words where you will draw your own line in the sand.

Check that you are acting from the best possible motives and not because you are allowing yourself to be victimized. Review the situation and your feelings. If you are saying 'yes' but you experience fear, anger, intimidation, resentment, irritation, helplessness, or low self-esteem, then it is time for you to draw a new line in the sand. Create a new boundary line – I will go this far and no further. You can be a good friend and still say 'no'.

Look for a new experience

23   Look for a new experience

Do something different, something that you have never done before. Go to a concert to hear some music that is new to you; sign up for a pottery class; eat vegetarian food; learn a new language; visit a place where you have never been . . . The possibilities are endless. When we do something for the first time we always experience a change of energy and we learn something new about ourselves.

Looking for something new encourages our natural curiosity, inquisitiveness and interest. Young children have a natural interest in anything new; they actively pursue new activities and this is how they learn about their world. Unfortunately as we grow older we often lose this interest in life, and low self-esteem brings boredom and fatigue. Re-awaken your interest by looking for something new to experience. An adventurous spirit encourages creativity, excitement and good feelings about ourselves and others.

Get in touch with nature

24   Get in touch with nature

The natural world is a great balm for troubled minds. Many of us live a fast-paced lifestyle surrounded by the gadgets of modern technology. Crowded towns and cities, high levels of pollution and a society of car drivers create many social problems. When we are high in self-esteem our minds are at peace, and one of the most effective ways to calm the mind is to get in touch with the natural world.

Plan to escape the town or city even if it can only be for a few hours a week. If this is impossible, then take a walk in the park. Take time to appreciate the wonders of nature: the colour of the sky, the green of the grass, the beauty of flowers, the songs of the birds. Slow down for a while and enjoy some peace and quiet.

It's surprising how quickly we can restore ourselves in this way. Low self-esteem may be just the result of trying too hard and too fast to keep up with the pressures of modern life. Take a natural break and enjoy the simple pleasures, and restore yourself and your self-esteem.

Manage your time

25 Manage your time

If you lead a busy life and you don't organize your time, then sooner or later your busyness will overwhelm you. I know someone who created a serious sleep problem for herself because she didn't manage her time effectively. She had three children and worked full time and just 'muddled along'. She started to wake up with panic attacks and then be unable to get back to sleep. She traced the panic to a feeling of being 'out of control' of her life, and she spent many nights worrying about things she 'should' have done or 'must remember' to do. This is a common syndrome which easily develops as our responsibilities grow.

Happily there is an easy solution – time management. Your desire to make the best use of your time depends upon how much you value it. If you own time is valuable to you, then start to manage it.

EXERCISE – TIME MANAGEMENT

1 Write things down, create lists of things to do, use a pinboard, use a diary.
2 Look at the lists, pinboard and diary!
3 Prioritize your jobs. Do you really need to do everything on your list? If not, delete those items.
4 Stop procrastinating – do the worst jobs of the day first. If you keep putting things off you will lose self-respect.
5 Say 'no' to things you can't or don't want to do and say it at once. Don't spend time worrying about how you are going to (eventually) back out.
6 Take time out for yourself in the spaces in the day that you have created by good time management. Don't just take on more work to fill in the gaps!

When you manage your time effectively you have a value on your time and effort. You will feel high in self-esteem and others will treat you with more respect.

Give yourself some 'feeling checks'

26 Give yourself some 'feeling checks'

Our feelings are very important, but sometimes we deny them because we are afraid of what people might think of us. Have you ever done this?

Our society does not encourage us to express our feelings, and men usually have more trouble than women in this area. How many men do you know who are able to talk about their feelings? You may be in a close relationship with someone who has denied their feelings for so long that they don't even know what they are feeling any more. It is very common for me to ask a client how they are feeling and for them to reply that they 'don't know'. People who are out of touch with their feelings are not being true to themselves and so they are low in self-esteem.

EXERCISE

Give yourself some 'feeling checks' throughout the day. This means that whenever you remember, stop for a moment and ask yourself, 'What am I feeling now?' As you practise this technique you will become more and more aware of your feelings. You are learning to listen with your heart.

Recognize your needs by getting in touch with your feelings and your self-esteem will rise.

Scream your head off

27   Scream your head off

It has been a difficult day. Everyone was late getting up and you had to rush to get the children to school, then you were late for work and realized you had left an important file at home, then the tea machine stopped working, then the babysitter phoned to say that she couldn't make it tonight, and then . . . . Whatever sequences of events or people have come together to create tension in your life, how are you going to deal with it?

We all know what it feels like to be tense, and when we feel it we are certainly not at our rational best. Tension leads inevitably to explosion, often inappropriate explosion. The person you finally scream at has usually had absolutely nothing to do with the small stress-inducing items that have built up to create your volcano of anger. Before you reach the point of explosion do the following exercise.

EXERCISE

Go and find a quiet and private spot. Stretch your mouth as wide as you can and tense your facial, neck and head muscles. The rest of your body may feel pretty tense too. Then, clench your fists and beat the air and scream . . . silently!

Then relax totally and repeat the operation. Do this until you feel better. You may even find yourself moved to laughter!

Let go of stress as quickly as you can. It lowers your ability to take charge of your life and it lowers your self-esteem.

Replace the word 'problem' with the word 'challenge'

28 Replace the word 'problem' with the word 'challenge'

Next time you face a difficult situation try to think of it as a challenge rather than a problem. When we think that we face a problem we become stressed and worried and it can feel hard to find a solution.

Look at your difficulties in a new way. You are a powerful and creative person and you can rise to the challenges that life offers.

Instead of saying, 'I've got a problem'   (negative)
say,   'How can I face this challenge?' (positive).

It's surprising how the words we use can affect how we see a situation. The Chinese symbol for crisis is also the symbol for opportunity. What an interesting way of perceiving our difficulties! Instead of being 'problems' they become challenges to our inventiveness. They become opportunities for us to grow and develop and to increase our power to change things. When we know that we can be effective in the world we no longer feel victimized and our self-esteem increases.

Listen for a day

29   Listen for a day

Experience a day in a new way. Spend a day listening to everyone you meet rather than talking to them. Such an approach will change the whole focus of your day and will take you 'outside' of yourself. It is easy to forget to listen because it's not something that we are very conscious of in our society. Indeed listening has become a dying art.

Whenever we listen to people we are showing them that we value them and that we are interested in them, and this appreciation encourages them to feel good about themselves. Your family will respond to the increased attention and will have plenty to say and you will have made time to hear it.

The 'feeling good' benefits exist for everyone involved in the communications. The people you listen to feel valued and respected. The good feelings will be returned, and you will feel as if you have done a good job and so your own self-esteem will rise. When we are high in self-esteem we encourage others to feel their own self-worth.

We learn so much about ourselves by listening to others, you will probably want to do it again another day!

Ground yourself

30   Ground yourself

Low self-esteem can make us feel nervous and then we experience the physical symptoms of anxiety. Sweating, headaches, tense muscles, butterflies and the shakes only increase our poor feelings about ourselves. It is really important to be able to release stress and tension so that we can get back on top of things. One way to relax and to take back control is to physically 'ground' ourselves.

EXERCISE – GROUND YOURSELF

Take your mind away from the situation which is causing the stress. Become aware of your breathing and slow it down until you feel calmer. Sit with your back straight and your feet flat on the floor. Close your eyes and imagine that your feet are connected to the centre of the earth. Some people imagine iron rods running from the bottom of their feet right down into the earth. Others visualize roots connecting them. Use whatever image comes to mind. Breathe deeply and feel the pull of gravity from your stomach to your feet and so through your connecting links into the earth. When you are ready open your eyes and bring yourself slowly back into the room.

We are creatures of the earth, and that is where our roots lie. Sometimes we forget our true beginnings and then we become nervous, stressed and afraid. The earth will always offer its support. We only need to connect with it.

Make something happen

31 Make something happen

What is the difference between people who make things happen and those who just seem to have things happen to them? Why can one person create new directions for her or himself whilst another always seems to be the victim of circumstances? The difference lies in their ability to make decisions.

How do you feel about making decisions? Would you describe your decision-making powers as:

- Good
- Not so good
- Poor
- Can't decide

When we are low in self-esteem it is hard to trust our own judgement. One way to overcome this is to use IDA. IDA is a simple formula which you can use whenever you are uncertain about what to decide and therefore how to act. IDA represents the following process:

INTENTION ⎯⎯⎯⎯⎯▶ DECISION ⎯⎯⎯⎯⎯▶ ACTION

You cannot act if you can't decide how to act, and you can't make a decision unless you know what you intend to happen. To discover your intention ask yourself this question: 'What do I want to happen?' Write down your answers and decide how you need to change your behaviour, then change your behaviour by acting differently.

If you feel like one of life's victims and you want to change, use IDA to become a person who can 'make something happen' and so increase your feelings of self-esteem.

61

Look in the mirror

32 Look in the mirror

Look in the mirror, look deeply into your own eyes and tell yourself how much you love and value yourself. You might use your name:

I (name) love and value myself

Repeat this whilst watching yourself. Make the exercise as meaningful as possible. This is really the most powerful way of making affirmations and it can be very confronting. If this is too difficult then write the affirmation twenty times. If you experience negative thoughts, turn the page over and write them on the back. As you begin to release such thoughts as 'This is stupid', 'This will never work', 'I don't deserve love', it will become easier to work with the mirror.

Eventually you will be able to use a mirror for all of your affirmations. Mirror work moves the energy faster. If you really want to be high in self-esteem and that is your goal, then persevere with this technique.

Start some physical exercise

33 Start some physical exercise

I know, this is your least favourite tip of all. You probably
have read all the others and have left this one until last.
However, regular exercise is a great self-esteem booster and
is probably one of the easiest ways to gain confidence in our
bodies and our abilities. Don't you feel really good about
yourself when you have had some exercise?

Take heart. I'm not going to suggest weight-training
twice a week or a five-mile jog or a fifty-length swim every
day or any other impossible feat. We often make unrealistic
promises in the keep-fit department, and then when we
don't keep them we feel bad about ourselves and our self-
esteem plummets even further. So let's keep our goals
realistic, because initially our sense of achievement is
maybe the only thing that can keep us going.

Begin with three ten-minute sessions for the following
week. If you are unused to exercising, start with small goals
like walking short distances instead of driving or catching
the bus (environmentally friendly and cost-cutting as well
as being good for you). Small achievements will develop
your inclination and motivation to increase your regular
physical activity, and once you start to really enjoy the
benefits there will be no stopping you!

Forgive someone

34   Forgive someone

The state of forgiveness increases self-esteem.
The state of unforgiveness decreases self-esteem.

Forgiveness is a powerful way of increasing our self-esteem. When I first suggest to people that they might forgive someone with whom they are angry, they usually say, 'Why should I after what they did to me?'

Forgiveness does not mean that we think that it's OK for anybody to do anything to us. Forgiveness is all about letting go. If I cannot forgive you then my angry thoughts will connect me to you forever. You may live ten thousand miles away, but if all I have to do is think of you and my emotions are all stirred up then I might as well be living with you. And so it is that we can be bound in hatred all our lives to someone whom we may never see. We may even be carrying anger for someone who has died. This is not at all unusual.

Is there someone you find it difficult to forgive? If so, ask yourself what you gain from not forgiving this person.

You gain a permanent relationship with this person. You are bound together by anger. Is this what you really want? Forgiving does not mean overlooking, it means the opposite. Before you can let go of the ties that bind you to another person in hatred, you need to know exactly what hurt you and why and then you need to express this in an appropriate way. When you can truly forgive, you set yourself free. How can you be high in self-esteem if you are hating someone?

Expect the best

35 Expect the best

Our thoughts are very powerful. By changing our thoughts we can change the quality of our lives, we can create low or high self-esteem for ourselves. How does this work?

Imagine that you have woken up feeling low. 'Oh no,' you think, 'this is going to be a bad day.' You start the day expecting the worst to happen – and it will! You feel grumpy, you look grumpy. Who wants to communicate with you in that mood? If anything good comes along you will miss it because you aren't expecting it or no one can be bothered to tell you about it. Start the day again. You wake up feeling low but you know how to change your mood. 'I'm feeling a bit low but I know that it's going to be a good day.' And it will be. It will definitely be better than your first try. You smile and try to lift your spirits, and those around you respond to you. You are high in expectation, so when that great opportunity presents itself you will recognize it.

A negative attitude attracts negative people and events into your life. Expect the worst and it will happen; you will 'prove' your expectations to be true. 'You see, I told you it would be a terrible day and it was.'

Positivity attracts positivity. Birds of a feather flock together. Expect the best and it will happen. Tomorrow morning when you wake up, say 'I know that this will be a good day.' Give it a try, expect the best *all day*, and see what happens.

Breathe deeply

36 Breathe deeply

The Basic Breath will help you to increase your composure, whatever the situation. The way we breathe actually affects the way we think, feel and act. Most of us breathe between twelve and eighteen times a minute. If you can reduce your breaths to eight a minute or less, this will automatically increase your feelings of self-respect and self-control.

EXERCISE – THE BASIC BREATH

1 Sit on the edge of a chair, back straight and feet on the floor. Hold your hands around your lower abdomen, one each side of your stomach, with the backs of your hands resting on your thighs.
2 Exhale fully with a loud sigh. Deflate your stomach down to your groin and hold it empty for a few seconds.
3 Start to inhale very slowly, with your mouth closed and feel your lower abdomen swelling in your hands. Visualize the area from your groin to your rib cage as a beautiful coloured balloon and watch it inflate slowly, filling from the bottom (imagine the air coming from between your legs). Expand your balloon fully and hold for three seconds.
4 Exhale slowly, watching the balloon deflate, until your abdomen is flat.
5 Repeat. (Start with ten slow breaths.)

Slow and complete breathing calms and oxygenates the system, removes the build-up of toxins in the body, lowers your heart and pulse rate and your cholesterol levels, as well as increasing your levels of self-esteem! Give it a try. You can even do this one sitting at your desk at work.

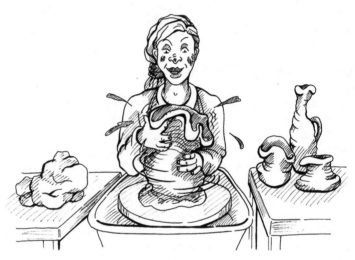

Create something

37   Create something

When we are low in self-esteem we lose interest in life, nothing seems worth doing and we feel low in energy. Re-awaken your interest and motivation and get your creative juices flowing again by creating something. Decide upon a project, however small, and then go ahead and be creative. Some possibilities are:

- Make and decorate a cake
- Prepare a special meal
- Plant some seeds
- Undertake any gardening project
- Arrange some flowers
- Create any handicraft – knitting/woodwork/sewing, etc.
- Write a letter to someone you love
- Paint a wall, a room, a picture.

There are many things that we can do to break the negative cycle of low self-esteem. The possibilities are endless. It's amazing how quickly our interest in life can be recaptured when we encourage ourselves to be creative. A creative project helps to still the mind and restore self-respect. Try it, it really is great therapy.

Be true to yourself

38   Be true to yourself

Sometimes we are not entirely truthful with ourselves. Perhaps we are finding it difficult to accept the truth and so we deny it. Maybe we are doing something that we feel we 'should' do but it doesn't feel right. We might even be doing something we don't want to do just so that we don't have to 'rock the boat'. If you are feeling uncomfortable in any area of your life, look inside yourself and closely examine your motives. Ask yourself the following questions:

- Am I being honest with myself?
- If not, then why not?
- Am I trying to please someone?
- If so, why?
- Am I afraid to say 'no' to this person?
- What is the worst thing that can happen to me if I stand up for myself and do what I want to do?
- What is it that I want to do?

If we live a lie, we will always be low in self-respect. Be true to yourself always and you will be high in self-esteem.

Watch your body language

39   Watch your body language

Our body language reflects what we are feeling. If we are low in self-esteem our shoulders droop, we avoid eye contact and our body signals that we don't wish to communicate with others. These body messages clearly tell people how we are feeling about ourselves.

If we change our body messages so that they are more assertive we will increase our self-esteem. Next time you are feeling low, sit up straight with your shoulders back and start to maintain eye contact with others. (This physical shift alone can start to move you out of your negativity.) Then change your body signals so that it is obvious that you are open to communicating with others. Put a smile on your face, make some physical contact, and the new assertive-looking you will indeed become more assertive.

As low self-esteem is reflected in our body language, so too is high self-esteem. If we look more assertive we feel more assertive and others will respond to our new feelings of self-respect.

Write your action plan

40   Write your action plan

Whatever your goals you can bring them closer by writing an action plan. When we commit ourselves on paper we take ourselves much more seriously. Choose a relatively short-term goal, write an action plan which will describe how you are to attain your goal, and then activate your plan. When you specify a goal and then put your own action plan to work your self-esteem will soar. Sometimes the plan won't work and you will need to make changes, but this doesn't matter. Action planning will demonstrate to you that you really do create your own reality and this is a very empowering feeling.

EXERCISE

Divide a piece of paper into five columns with the following headings:

INTENTION   METHOD   NEEDS   REVIEW   ANY CHANGES

Intention: State an objective. I want to: ....
Method: Decide what steps you need to take. List them in order.
Needs: List all the resources you may need, e.g. help, advice, finance, family support . . . Your list may change as time passes.
Review: Give yourself some realistic deadlines. Decide on certain dates to look at your progress.
Any changes: Note any changes that will be needed. This is your flexibility column and will affect the rest of your plan. Be prepared to adapt your plan so you respond creatively to change instead of being floored by the first hiccup.

Action plans for the short term lead to confidence and self-esteem to plan for more ambitious and far-reaching goals.

Speak well of others

41 Speak well of others

When we speak badly about other people we change the way that we feel about ourselves. Have you ever listened to anyone gossiping about someone else, saying bad things about them? How do you feel about the person who is gossiping? Are you comfortable with people who talk about others behind their back? Could you trust such a person? Could they be a good friend to you?

Next time you find yourself speaking badly about others, notice what you are doing. Do you need to say these things? Will it change anything for the better? If it won't then stop! Remember how you feel about others who gossip? Well, this is how you will feel about yourself if you start. Negativity creates bad feeling and never leads to constructive change. Those who feel badly about themselves are the ones who gossip about other people. Those who respect themselves treat other people in a respectful manner. Look for something positive to say about those around you and you will find your own energy improving and your self-respect and self-esteem increasing.

Say 'no' when you want to

42 Say 'no' when you want to

'No' is such a small word, but it seems to be one of the hardest words for us to say. A client once told me that she was ten years into her marriage before she could tell her husband that 'no' she didn't like having her hair stroked. When they first met her husband had loved to stroke her hair and he had asked her if she liked it too. She had said 'yes' when she really meant 'no' because she wanted to please him. It wasn't until after the birth of her third child that she told her husband her true feelings. He was amazed that she hadn't hold him sooner.

If you are saying 'yes' when you really want to say 'no' then you are not saying what you mean and this will affect your feelings of self-respect. We all struggle with this little word as we find ourselves doing all sorts of things that we don't really want to do. If we don't say 'no' when we want to, we do things with anger and resentment and our self-esteem falls rapidly.

Practice saying 'no'. Say it out loud to yourself when there's no one around, just to get used to saying it. Then imagine the situation where you would like to say it. See the person in your mind's eye and visualize yourself saying 'no' to them. Practice makes perfect! The first time you say your 'no' for real it might feel a bit scary. Don't apologize after you say it, just congratulate yourself! The next time it will be easier. Whenever you are feeling victimized, you are low in self-esteem and you need to say 'no' to somebody. Say 'no' when you want to and you will feel proud of yourself.

Let go of guilt

43   Let go of guilt

Guilt destroys self-esteem. It's like a strong acid which burns away self-respect. Women have a close relationship with irrational guilt, living with such brain teasers as: 'Am I a good enough mother?' 'Am I a good enough wife?' 'If I don't work we won't have enough money, if I do work I can't spend so much time with the children.' Wracked with guilt we have been known to fly from pillar to post trying to be all things to everybody, always in a no-win situation and with our self-esteem getting lower and lower.

If this is you then stop for a moment. Guilt will destroy your self-esteem unless you decide to erase it from your life. There are no half measures here; guilt cannot even be a casual visitor. Children are very quick to pick up on guilt and move swiftly in to make extra demands when they sense the merest hint of it.

EXERCISE – LETTING GO OF GUILT

Make the affirmation, *I am always doing my best*, whilst visualizing any guilty feelings floating away in a bubble, never to be seen again. And then let go. Don't think about it again.

Remember that if you are allowing yourself to feel guilt you will be low in self-esteem; this is the only reward you will get! Keep practising letting go of guilt and it will get easier and easier to do as your life gets easier and easier to live.

Balance yourself

44   Balance yourself

When we are feeling high in self-esteem our mind, body, spirit and emotions are balanced. If our lives become out of balance in some way then our self-esteem will fall. If, for example, I spend the whole of today thinking and writing this book (mental activity), then by bedtime I will be wound up and feeling physically uncomfortable. If I spend the whole day analysing my feelings about having to get the book finished (emotional activity), then there will have been no action and no writing and I will be panicking at bedtime! I could spend the whole day walking (physical activity), good exercise if I need it and have no deadline to meet. However, if I walk all day the job will not be done and I will be anxious. I could meditate and visualize that the book will be written in time (spiritual activity), a good tactic but not on its own – it needs to be supported by real action.

We are built for mental, physical, emotional and spiritual activity. Creativity and high self-esteem depend upon the balance of these activities. If you are feeling less than your best, check to see if you are in balance by asking the following questions:

- How much mental activity have I had today?
- How much physical activity have I had today?
- How long have I been in touch with my emotions today?
- How much spiritual activity have I had today?

Discover where the imbalance lies and then look through this book to find the ways you need to re-create balance and self-esteem in your life.

Trust your intuition

45   Trust your intuition

When we are feeling good and we are high in self-esteem our energies are balanced, our hearts and minds are working together, and we are in touch with both our logic and our intuition.

We have all been taught to be logical, to use our minds to 'reason things out', but as we know, our minds cannot provide all the answers. Life is not just a rational process. Our intuition is also involved.

Can you trust your intuition? Do you know what it is and do you know where to look for it?

You are tapping into your intuition when you have a 'hunch' about something; when you 'know' that something is true even if you haven't been told about it. Your intuition gives you important information and speaks to you through urges, feelings and flashes of insight. Do you remember a time when you just *knew* what to do (it was a gut feeling) and you did it and things turned out well? That was your intuition at work.

Listen to your intuition, trust what it tells you, and you will become more alive, spontaneous and balanced and your feelings of self-worth and self-respect will increase.

Make an appreciation list

46 Make an appreciation list

If you are feeling low, then find something to appreciate, however small it might be. No matter how depressed you feel, there will always be something that you can appreciate. Go and look for it! Find it! When all is bleak and your life has lost its zap, make an appreciation list. You may have to search hard but I promise that it will be worth it. The act of appreciation waters your seeds of self-esteem.

EXERCISE

Make a list like the one below. List as many things as you can.

MY APPRECIATION LIST

I (your name) . . . . .appreciate . . . .

I . . . . .appreciate . . . .

I . . . . .appreciate . . . .

I . . . . .appreciate . . . .

Learn to be

47   Learn to be

We are all so busy running about doing this and doing that. Sometimes this feels good and gives us a sense of purpose, but activity alone can become meaningless and pointless. Excessive 'doing' can lead us to feel that we are running around a hamster's wheel and that we cannot get off. There is a relentless quality to this feeling. To lead a balanced life with inner strength and self-esteem we need to be able to step off the hamster's wheel when 'doing' becomes too much. We need times to just 'be'. Learning to relax, to stop 'doing' and to just 'be' increases our self-awareness and helps us to release tension.

EXERCISE

Spend a few minutes every day in silence. Turn off the television or radio. Don't read a book or 'do' anything, just sit in the peace and 'be'. This might be quite difficult at first so don't sit for too long. As you get used to 'being' the feeling will grow on you and you will be able to balance your 'being' with your 'doing'. This will increase your sense of purpose and self-esteem.

Focus on your strengths

48   Focus on your strengths

When our self-esteem is low we only see our weaknesses; if we make a mistake it just 'proves' how stupid and useless we are. There seems to be a natural tendency for us to bring ourselves down rather than to lift ourselves up. Perhaps we have been taught not to 'brag' about ourselves; not to 'show off'; to be modest. Personal levels of self-esteem *never* depend on what other people are thinking. Self-esteem depends only upon what we think about ourselves, and so if we bring ourselves down then that is exactly where we will stay – down.

We need to build ourselves up. This doesn't mean bragging and showing off, it means being quietly assertive. We all have weaknesses, but we can only change if we feel motivated and energetic. Negativity breeds depression and low energy levels. Positivity brings interest, motivation and the power to make changes. Forget about false modesty. Look to your strengths. What are you good at? These things can be big or small, it doesn't matter.

EXERCISE

When you are low in self-esteem, lift yourself out of depression by focusing on your strengths. Make a list of them.

MY STRENGTHS ARE

1 . . . .

2 . . . .

Write down as many as you can think of. Read them out loud. Be proud of your abilities. Self-respect opens the door to self-esteem.

Let go of your suppressed feelings

49   Let go of your suppressed feelings

Many of us have been taught from a very early age that our feelings are best kept to ourselves. If we have become good at hiding our feelings (unexpressed feelings), we may reach a stage where we are even able to hide our feelings from ourselves (unacknowledged feelings). However, hidden feelings don't go away – they have to be hidden somewhere. We hide them inside ourselves and they cause us pain and misery and low self-esteem.

Learn to accept all your feelings. It really is OK to feel angry, jealous, selfish, afraid … and all those other emotions which we have been taught are 'bad'. Feelings will never go away unless we feel them through, and then we can release them. Start to love your feelings, experience them to the full, and then let go of them with your self-esteem intact.

EXERCISE

1 Acknowledge your feeling, give it a name.
2 Accept that you have this feeling.
3 Allow yourself to feel this emotion all the way through. It may take some time to go through this process.
4 Imagine all the parts of this emotion encased within a bubble.
5 Let that bubble float away.

Go on holiday

50   Go on holiday

Your life is busy and it seems everyone is making demands, so when can you get some time to yourself? Do you ever feel like this? Perhaps you need to look at your time management, but in the short term here's a little quick relaxer.

EXERCISE – GOING ON HOLIDAY

When you *do* have about thirty minutes to spare find a quiet private place and sit down and relax. Close your eyes and become aware of your breathing. When your mind and body are feeling deeply relaxed, create, in your mind's eye, a beautiful scene. Choose an outdoor setting, by the beach, in the mountains, in a garden, whenever you like. Fill the scene with colour and detail, create your own wonderful holiday brochure photograph. Absorb the details of this place, see the sights, smell the fragrances, hear the birdsong, the running water, the waves crashing on the rocks. When you have created your ideal spot slowly return into the room and open your eyes.

Now you can go on holiday whenever you like. It only takes a second to get there, there's no packing and it's free. You can go at any time in any situation. When the going gets rough close your eyes for a few seconds, visualize your dream place and just be there. You really can 'get away from it all' and come back feeling refreshed without anyone ever knowing that you left.

Perfect this technique. It really is fantastic!

Start today to make your dreams come true

51 Start today to make your dreams come true

Have you ever heard people say things like: I've always wanted to go there, do that, have one of those, visit that place, start that business, begin that hobby? Why didn't they ever do these things? When we know what we would love to do, we can start taking steps towards our goals. Do the exercise below to discover your goals.

EXERCISE – TEN THINGS I WANT TO DO IN MY LIFE

I want:

To ....

To ....

To ....

To ....

To ....

To ....

To ....

To ....

To ....

To ....

Are you taking steps towards doing any of these things? If not, why not? Focus on the steps you need to take to achieve your goals. Don't be a person who complains that they never got what they wanted out of life or you will always be disappointed and have low self-respect. Reach for the stars, take a risk, be courageous and *act*. Your self-esteem will rise in direct proportion to the personal risks that you are prepared to take.

Create success for yourself

52   Create success for yourself

Your imagination is very powerful, it can create whatever it chooses. Decide to create success for yourself. Say the following affirmation:

AFFIRMATION: I deserve success

Now use your imagination to reinforce this affirmation.

EXERCISE – VISUALIZATION

Find a comfortable place, close your eyes and relax. Follow your breathing until you feel deeply relaxed and then *see* your success in action. Picture the scene that you would like to create. See yourself being a successful – You look so confident and relaxed. Feel what it is like to be a success. See people treating you with the respect that you deserve. Make the vision as real as you can: see and hear the whole thing in glorious technicolour, create the sound effects, feel the reality of your success. When you are ready let your thoughts return, open your eyes and come back into the room.

If you have negative thoughts when you are visualizing, just let them go. This technique is very powerful and in fact it is one that we use frequently. We often use our imagination in a negative way to support negative beliefs about ourselves. Have you ever thought that you would like to try something and then quickly decided not to bother because you wouldn't be able to do it?

What has happened here is that you used a negative affirmation – a belief that 'I can't do that'. This was supported by a negative visualization, when in your imagination you saw yourself failing. So you see we use these techniques all the time. Why not use them to create positivity, success and high self-esteem?

Teach your children well

53 Teach your children well

Our negative beliefs stand between us and our self-esteem. We learned these beliefs in our childhood. We know so much today about the power of positive thinking and the results of negative criticism. For those of us who are parents this knowledge is invaluable. Words are so powerful and they can be used to encourage and support or to belittle and tease. We know that babies and tiny children believe what we teach them to believe. If they are told that they are stupid, useless, no good, worthless, lazy, etc., they will believe these things to be true about themselves and they will grow up with little confidence and low self-esteem, which inevitably leads to poor behaviour patterns.

With the knowledge and awareness that we now possess, we can encourage and empower our children by supporting them in a positive way. This does not mean that we tell them that everything they do is marvellous – far from it. We can admire our children and tell them how much we love them and how clever they are. We can encourage them to discuss their feelings about things, and we can show them ways to do things without belittling their own attempts. I'm not talking about 'perfect parenting' here. We can only ever do our best and that may often seem 'wrong'. Parenting is hard, but we know how to give our children a positive start in life so that they will have respect for themselves and others.

Each time you encourage a person to increase their self-esteem your own sense of value increases. Empower your children and help to secure a generation of young people who are high in self-esteem.

Remember that you are unique

54 Remember that you are unique

Do you ever compare yourself with other people? Do you ever feel that you are 'not as good as' someone else, or not sufficiently clever/thin/beautiful/worthy/happy? Each time you compare yourself with someone else you are mistrusting your own ability to make decisions and choices, you are behaving like a victim with low self-esteem.

You are unique. There never has and there never will be another person on the planet who is just like you. This makes you original and special. Make the following affirmation:

AFFIRMATION: I am unique

Say this over and over. Say it out loud to yourself.

Enhance your originality. Whenever you feel the urge to 'fit in', look carefully at whatever you feel it is that makes you different. Accept and make the most of your differences. They are what make you a unique and original person with your own special place in the world.

Do the 'You can't make me' swing

55 Do the 'You can't make me' swing

Children have natural ways to reduce stress which we forget as we grow up. Get in touch with your childish playfulness and rebelliousness and enjoy the following exercise, which has a really effective de-stressing and calming influence.

EXERCISE – THE 'YOU CAN'T MAKE ME' SWING

Stand with your feet apart (about the width of your shoulders). Swing your body, neck and head as one unit to the left and then to the right. Let your arms swing freely as your body turns from side to side, so that they wrap round you at your shoulders. Make sure that your head follows your body as you swing.

As your body swings from left to right and back, shout 'You can't make me!' as loud as possible.

Enjoy yourself. Keep shouting. Try 'I don't care' or 'No I won't'.

Letting go of anger in this way is good for self-respect and also introduces a humorous touch. When we are low in self-esteem we are inclined to take ourselves far too seriously. So swing, shout and laugh and bring everything back into perspective.

Step into a bubble

56   Step into a bubble

A long time ago, before I began my search for ways to feel better about myself, I was in a very low state. I was in the middle of a severe personal trauma and I had no self-belief. In fact I had no belief in anything. When we are in the depths of despair and suffer from low self-esteem we lose all sense of trust in ourselves and in other people, and so we feel lonely, vulnerable and afraid. This feeling of vulnerability can make us feel exposed and unprotected and very sensitive to others. Whilst in this exposed state I met someone who revealed to me a most amazing yet simple visualization technique which I used to strengthen and protect myself.

EXERCISE – YOUR BUBBLE OF LIGHT

Close your eyes and relax in a comfortable position and become aware of your breathing. Slowly follow your breaths in and out, in and out. Concentrate on the rhythm of your breathing until you are feeling very relaxed. Now, imagine yourself standing in front of an open window. You see a beautiful bubble come floating through the window. Notice the colour of your bubble. The bubble floats to the floor in front of you and, as you watch, it grows in size and beauty until it is bigger than you. Now step into your bubble. You are feeling totally protected. You know that nothing and no one can harm you when you are inside your beautiful bubble.

Use this technique whenever you feel the need. You can visualize your bubble and step into it as quickly as blinking. Try it, practise it, and feel the wonderful protection it offers.

Be assertive

57 Be assertive

We teach people the way we want them to treat us. This means that if people are using you as a doormat then this is because you have let them do so. If you are low in self-esteem, then someone in your life will be victimizing you. Look closely at your relationships, whether with your partner, friends, work colleagues or family. Ask yourself these questions:

• Who am I allowing to treat me badly?
• How am I allowing this to happen?

Change this relationship by changing your own behaviour. Act assertively and your victimizers will either change the way they behave towards you or they will leave your life.

• Know what you want and respect your own wishes.
• Believe that you can make things happen – and then do it!
• Don't be afraid to say 'no' whenever you need to.
• Use good communication skills.
• Don't be afraid to take a chance – life is full of risks.
• Accept responsibility for your own actions.
• Express your true feelings.

A non-victim response is an assertive response. You are being assertive when you act in your own best interests and stand up for yourself. You communicate your needs clearly and also respect the rights and feelings of other people. You value yourself and are high in self-esteem.

Make a list of positive affirmations

58 Make a list of positive affirmations

Your self-esteem is based on your self-belief. When the going gets rough it is often difficult to maintain our self-belief. If we are low it feels impossible to believe that we really are special, worthy and lovable. But of course it is always true. It is at these times of difficulty that we most need to believe in ourselves. Belief is very strong magic! When it feels impossible to love yourself, then practise. Practise believing that you are amazing, important, wonderful, creative, deserving, significant – because you are.

EXERCISE

Create your own list of affirming self-beliefs. Keep these affirmations in the present tense; keep them positive and practise saying them, all the time. Refer to your list as soon as you feel your self-esteem falling. Use the examples below if you wish and create some more of your own.

EXAMPLES
'I love and value myself'
'I am a wonderful and creative person'
'I deserve the best in life'

MY LIST OF POSITIVE AFFIRMATIONS

1 ....

2 ....

3 ....

Break a habit

59 Break a habit

One of the effects of low self-esteem is a feeling of 'stuckness': of not being able to change anything for the better and so feeling out of control. For some people this feeling escalates until they become severely depressed. In order to feel good about our lives we need to feel that we have some control, and if we become lost in a dark place which is full of negativity it can feel as if we have lost all control.

The smallest steps we take can have the greatest impact upon our lives. If you are feeling lost and don't know which way to turn, just decide to change something about your life. Choose something which appears to be very small and insignificant. Break a minor habit. Don't try to do anything drastic like stopping smoking or ending a relationship. We are looking for a small change here, one that will not cost much energy but that will instigate some change in your life. Change your route to work; put the toilet paper on the holder in the opposite way; buy some different bread; change your hairstyle.

As you start to do things differently you will recognize more and more habitual behaviour patterns that you can change. Self-change, even in small ways, starts a process that can pull you out of negativity as new possibilities emerge on the horizon. Remember that you *can* change your life and you *can* create self-esteem, however impossible this may seem to you at the moment.

Congratulate yourself

60 Congratulate yourself

Congratulate yourself for recognizing your power to change the quality of your life. When you bought this book you took the biggest step towards self-esteem that you will ever have to take. The rest only requires practice. When you are feeling low, too low to bother with my 60 tips for self-esteem, remember that you are not alone. We are all working towards greater self-awareness.

As you learn to increase your self-esteem, you will also enhance the lives of others. The quality of your life affects everyone around you, so go ahead and create an abundance of self-esteem for everyone to share.

This work is not always easy. Sometimes it feels impossible to believe in yourself. Never doubt that you are progressing in your quest for self-esteem and know that all the love and support you need will always be with you.